The A-Z of 13 Habits

D1500463

Noela

your love inspired me

"The message is not about the money, as much as it is about attitudes, behaviors and thought processes that relate to the resources around us — money, the planet, home, friends and so on," says Dr. John Hattie, Professor of Education, Director of Visible Learning Labs.

"These 'big and rich' habits can be understood by even the youngest of children. To see children afire with ideas and questions after hearing the story and to see them make connections to their lives — these are the art of a true story teller."
Professor John Hattie

"A child will want to pick this up.
I don't care if they are 8 years old,
18 years old or 80 years old!"
Beth Black, The Book Worm, Omaha, Nebraska

The A-Z of 13 Habits

Shareholder Letters by Warren Buffett: www.berkshirehathaway.com/letters/letters.html

Story and Creative Direction by Lucas Remmerswaal: www.lucasremmerswaal.com

Original Art and illustrations by Annette Lodge: www.annettelodge.com

Concept development layout and design by Karl Fountaine: www.fountainedesign.co.nz

Title: The tale of Tortoise Buffett and Trader Hare
Author: Lucas Remmerswaal
Publisher: Lucas Remmerswaal
Address: 57 Crawford Cres, Kamo, Whangarei
ISBN-13: 13: 978-1461016212
ISBN-10: 1461016215

I met Warren Buffett at Piccolo Pete's, one of his favorite restaurants in Omaha. When I approached his table I said to him: "I'm Lucas Remmerswaal from New Zealand. I've spent the last nine months creating 6 books for children about your habits."

Buffett chuckled and said to me, "I hope it's not my bad habits........."

Good habits once established are just as hard to break as bad habits! Start by reading the "13 Habits that made me Billions" today and simply remind yourself to read every day. In just 21 days, reading will become one of your good habits.
– Lucas Remmerswaal

13 Habits that made me Billions

Inspired by Warren Buffett

Lucas Remmerswaal
Illustrated by Annette Lodge

Look out for
our next book
in the series...

13HABITS.COM

Chains of habit are
too light to be felt
until they are too
heavy to be broken.

These are the bottles of Coca-Cola
Warren Buffett, also known as Fireball,
sold to earn money when he was six
years old. Now Berkshire Hathaway
owns 8.6% of the Coca-Cola Company.

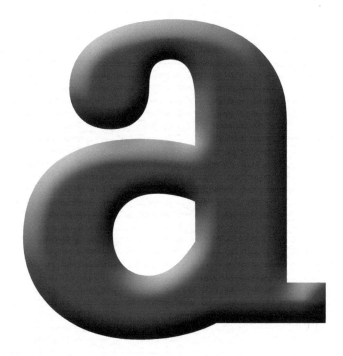

is for Assiduity

Be persistent and apply yourself
to your work and study.

is for Books

Join the library. Read everything you can!

is for
Compound Interest

Like a snowball your money can grow.

is for Dream

Think BIG and live the life of your dreams.

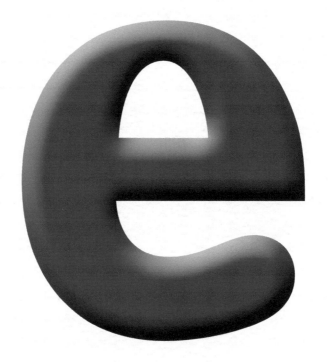

is for Energy

Energy is the essence of life.

is for Fun

Have fun! Enjoy the process more than the proceeds.

is for Giant Goals

Goals are simply dreams with a deadline.

is for Habit

Winners make a habit of doing the
things losers don't want to do.

is for Integrity

Integrity is doing the right thing when nobody's looking.
Be honest with yourself and others.

is for Just do it!

first you make your habits,
then your habits make you!

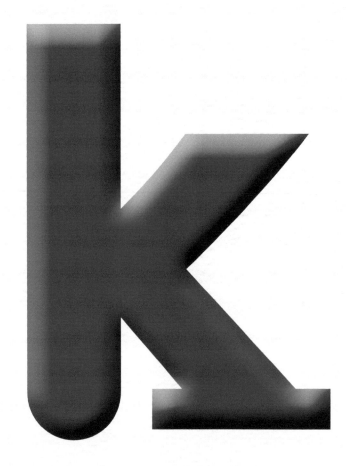

is for Knowledge

The application of knowledge is power - use it wisely.

is for Learn

Be a continuous learning machine.

is for Money

Avoid borrowed money!
Save at least 10% of everything you earn.

is for Notes

ACTION LIST

- ✓ List 10 things to do today
- ✓ Tick them off one at a time
- ✓ Write the next 10
- Do them 10 at the time
- Do it every day

Write notes to keep track of your thoughts.

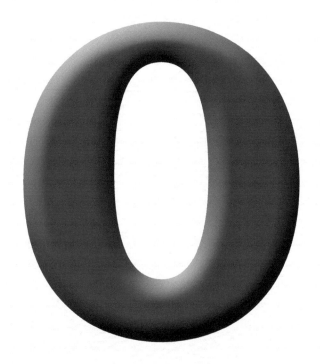

is for Occupy

Occupy your mind everyday with a book.
Absorb elementary worldly wisdom.

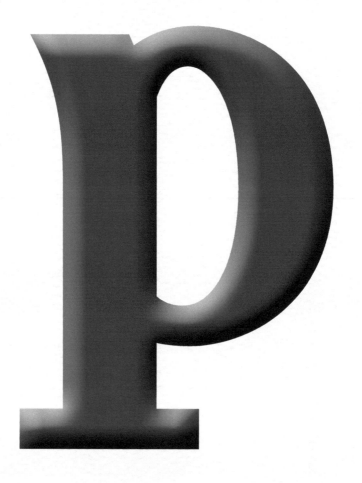

is for Persistence

Nothing in the world
can take the place of persistence.

Wishing will not; Talent will not;
Genius will not; Education will not.

Persistence is like a genie that creates
a magical force in your life.

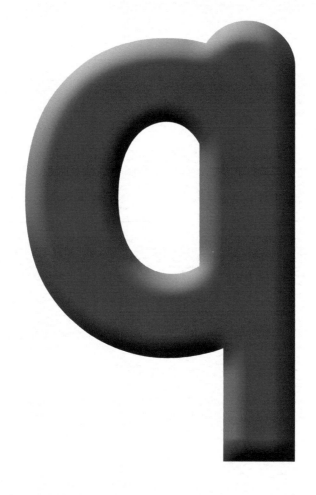

is for Quiet

Spend time everyday... to just sit... and think.

is for Read

Read everything you can with ferocious curiosity.

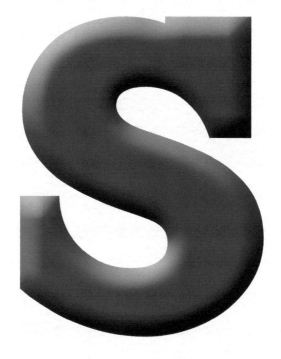

is for Scary

fear is driven out by Action!
Bad habits are overcome by good habits.

is for Think

Think outside the square. Think for yourself,
don't just follow the herd. Think multidisciplinary!
Problems by definition, cross many academic disciplines.

is for Understand

Understand the importance of what you are doing,
reading, thinking, your habits and friends.

is for Value

Value is what you get! Price is what you pay.

is for Waste

Waste not want not - reuse, recycle.
Don't waste time, money, energy.

is for Xmas

Concentrate your energies, your thoughts and your capital.
Put all your eggs in one basket and watch that basket,
then all your Christmases can come at once!

is for You

You are responsible for your own actions.
Be proud of what you do.

is for Zany

Master the zany habit of thinking backwards.
It will help you become a really great thinker!

13 Habits that made me Billions – inspired by Warren Buffett

1. Integrity – Keep your own internal score card.
Be honest with yourself and others. Judge every action
you take by the newspaper test.

2. Intelligence – Read everything you can with ferocious curiosity.
Be a multi-disciplinary learning machine.

3. Assiduity – Commit with a passion to your work and study.
Be enthusiastic, have fun, enjoy the process more than the proceeds.

4. Frugality – Save at least 10% of everything you earn.
Avoid borrowed money. Invest on a small scale – don't just read!

5. Accounting – Make sure you understand the language of practical
business life. Double entry bookkeeping was a hell of a good invention.

6. Read – You will be the same person in five years as you are
today except for the people you meet and the books you read.

7. Gratitude – Work with people you like, trust and admire. Make sure
you appreciate everything they do and you'll tap dance to work
every morning!

8. Vision – If I have seen a little further it is by standing on the shoulders of Giants.

9. Think – for yourself. Don't just follow the herd! Take care of the down side and the up side will take care of itself.

10. Focus – Concentrate; put all your eggs in one basket, and then watch that basket. Stay within your circle of competence. Apply a margin of Safety.

11. Compound Interest – Let the most powerful force in the universe work for you. Understand the difference between 5% and 15%, and the effect of inflation.

12. Inversion – The mental habit of thinking backward forces objectivity. It's a trick that works in algebra and it's a trick that works in life. If you don't, you'll never be a really good thinker.

13. Intuition – Listen to tiny hunches, feelings, or fleeting thoughts. They are like clouds in the sky but when you write them down in a notebook and act on them, they will become your most powerful habit.

"Chains of habit are too light to be felt until they are too heavy to be broken".
Warren Buffett, Chairman and CEO Berkshire Hathaway Inc.

Warren Buffett MBA Talk Part 1

A short little sermon on Youtube: http://www.youtube.com/watch?v=DFuxKpMFUjc

"You've all got the IQ to do well, you've all got all the initiative and energy to do well or you wouldn't be here and most of you will succeed in meeting your aspirations but in determining whether you succeed there's more to it than intellect and energy. And I'd like to talk for just a second about that. In fact there was a fellow. Pete Kiewit in Omaha, who used to say that he looked for three things in hiring people — he looked for integrity, intelligence and energy and he said that if that person didn't have the first two that the latter two would kill him because if they don't have integrity you want them dumb and lazy, you don't want them smart and energetic. I'd really like to talk about that first one because we know you've got the second two. Play along with me in a little game for just a second in terms of thinking about that question... you've gotten to know your classmates. Think for a moment that I granted you the right to buy 10% of one of your classmates for the rest of his or her lifetime. You can't pick one with a rich father, that doesn't count, I mean you've got to pick somebody who's going to do it on their own merit and I gave you an hour to think about it. Which one are you going to pick among all your classmates as to the one you want to own 10% of for the rest of their lifetime? Are you going to give them an IQ test, pick the one with the highest IQ? I doubt it. Are you going to pick the one with the best grades? I doubt it. You're not even going to pick the most energetic one necessarily or the one that displays the most initiative but you're going to be looking for qualitative factors in addition because everybody's got enough brains and enough energy and I would say that if you thought about it for an hour, decided who you're going to place that bet on, you'd probably pick the one who you responded the best to, the one that was going to have the leadership qualities, the one that was going to be able to get other people to carry out their interests and that would be the person who was generous and honest and who gave credit to other people even if, for their own ideas, all kinds of qualities like that. And you could write down those qualities that you admire in this other person, whoever you admire most in the class. And then I would throw in a hooker, I would say as part of owning 10% of this person, you had to be ready to go short 10% on somebody else in the class. That's more fun isn't it? And you think now, who do I want to go short on and again, you wouldn't pick the person with the lowest IQ. You would start thinking about the person who really turned you off for one reason or another. He or she would have various qualities quite apart from their academic achievement but they would also have various qualities and you don't want to be around them, and other people don't want to be around them. What were the qualities that lead to that? There'd be a whole bunch of things, you know, but it's the person who's egotistical, the person who's greedy, the person who's slightly dishonest, cuts corners – all of these qualities! You can write those down on the right hand side of the page.......As you looked at those qualities on the left and right hand side there is one interesting thing about them. It's not the ability to throw a football 60 yards; it's not the ability to run the 100-yard dash in 9.3. It's not being the best looking person in the class...they're all qualities that if you really want to have the ones on the left hand side you can have them. They're qualities of behavior, temperament and character that are achievable. They're not forbidden to anybody in this group. And if you look at the qualities on the right hand side, the ones that you find turn you off in other people there's not a quality there that you have to have. If you have it, you can get rid of it, and you can get rid of it a lot easier at your age than you can at my age because most behavior is habitual and they say the chains of habit are too light to be felt until they are too heavy to be broken. There's no question about it. I see people with self-destructive behavior patterns at my age or even ten or twenty years younger and they really are entrapped by them. They go around and they do things that turn off other people right and left and they don't need to be that way but by a certain point they get so that they can hardly change it. But at your age you can have any habits, any patterns of behavior that you wish, it's simply a question of which you decide and why not decide the ones that. Ben Graham did this and Ben Franklin did it before him but Ben Graham in his lower teens looked around and he looked at the people he admired and he said, "You know, I want to be admired, so why don't I just behave like them," and he found there was nothing impossible about behaving like them. And similarly he did the same thing on the reverse side in terms of getting rid of those qualities so I would suggest that if you write those qualities down and think about them for a little while, make them habitual, you will be the one that you want to buy 10% of when you get all through and the beauty of it is you already own 100% and you're stuck with it so you might as well be that person as somebody else. Well, that's a short little sermon."

Warren Buffett, Chairman and CEO Berkshire Hathaway Inc.

I am your constant companion.
I am your greatest helper or heaviest burden.
I will push you onward or drag you down to failure.
I am completely at your command.
Half of the things you do you might as well turn over
to me and I will do them - quickly and correctly.
I am easily managed - you must be firm with me.
Show me exactly how you want something done and
after a few lessons, I will do it automatically.
I am the servant of great people,
and alas, of all failures as well.
Those who are great, I have made great.
Those who are failures, I have made failures.
I am not a machine though
I work with the precision of a machine
plus the intelligence of a person.
You may run me for profit or run me for ruin -
it makes no difference to me.
Take me, train me, be firm with me, and
I will place the world at your feet.
Be easy with me and I will destroy you.
Who am I? I am Habit.

Thank You

To everyone who generously gave their time
to help support me in publishing this series
of books to them I am truly grateful!

To Warren Buffett for making the
Berkshire Hathaway Shareholders letters available.
http://www.berkshirehathaway.com/letters/letters.html

To students and teachers at Hurupaki Primary
and Kamo Intermediate School in Whangarei.
http://www.youtube.com/watch?v=F_M7054SpWO

To my wife Noela, my kids, my father, my mother,
my family, Annette Lodge, Prof. John Hattie, Helena Cullen,
Barbara-Lucy Hosken, Jasmine Horton, John Stellar,
Kate Romero-Stellar, Karl, Jacqui, Carmen, Hamish
at Fountaine Design, and the team at Amazon.com.

CPSIA information can be obtained
at www.ICGtesting.com
Printed in the USA
LVIW021431050612

284775LV00005B